Cheryl Saban's GUIDE TO A

Happy and Mindful Life

Cheryl Saban's GUIDE TO A

Happy and Mindful Life

RYLAND PETERS & SMALL
LONDON • NEW YORK

Originally published as three
different titles: *Recipe for a Good
Marriage*, *Recipe for a Happy Life*,
and *Soul Sisters*.

This combined edition first published
in 2017 by Ryland Peters & Small
20–21 Jockey's Fields
London WC1R 4BW
and
341 E 116th Street
New York, NY 10029
www.rylandpeters.com

10 9 8 7 6 5 4 3 2 1

ISBN 978-1-84975-864-2

Printed and bound in China.

A CIP record for this book is
available from the British Library.

Senior designer Toni Kay
Commissioning editor Annabel Morgan
Picture research Christina Borsi
Head of production Patricia Harrington

Art director Leslie Harrington
Editorial director Julia Charles
Publisher Cindy Richards

Contents

Man is fond of counting his troubles, but he does not count his joys.
If he counted them up as he ought to, he would see that every lot
has enough happiness provided for it.

FYODOR DOSTOEVSKY

Introduction

One often hears about the concept of mindfulness, and I wonder – do we really know what mindfulness means? As a reminder, I'll note for you here that the actual definition of mindfulness is: "The quality or state of being conscious or aware of something, and a mental state that can be achieved by focusing one's awareness on the present moment." How often do we do that? My guess is, not very often. We're either so busy fretting about the past, or agonizing over what might happen in the future, that we miss what's going on right here, right now.

Being mindful helps us pay attention to the present moment, to our thoughts and feelings, and to do so without judging ourselves for them. Many of us meditate to quiet our mind—to simply be in the moment. It's a challenge to be-here-now, but it's worth it. Because life, after all, is about moment after moment after moment.

While there is no fail-safe map, no golden ticket, and no gain without effort to this miracle we call life, there are certainly methods you can use to be happier, healthier, and more mindful about the way you live your life. After having completed more than 65 laps around the sun, I have learned a few things along the way that have helped me carve out a happier and more mindful life for myself. Within these pages, I hope you'll discover some ideas that might inspire you to live a happier and more mindful life as well.

A Recipe for a
Happy and Mindful Life

be optimistic ❧ NOURISH CLOSE RELATIONSHIPS

be content with who you are

HAVE GOALS AND AMBITIONS ❧ *be grateful*

give to others ❧ DISCOVER YOUR PASSIONS

practice random acts of kindness

IMPROVE YOUR TALENTS ❧ *be kind and encouraging*

forgive others and yourself ❧ TAKE REGULAR EXERCISE

mind your health and take care of yourself

NURTURE YOUR SPIRITUAL BELIEFS

attract positive experiences ❧ *know your self-worth*

EAT REASONABLY AND SLEEP DEEPLY

pray ❧ WRITE YOUR STORY ❧ *commune with nature*

LEARN POSITIVE COPING SKILLS

write in a journal ❧ EXPRESS GOOD INTENTIONS

meditate ❧ *laugh more* ❧ LOVE ❧ *choose happiness*

*Happiness is when what you think, what you say,
and what you do are in harmony.*

MOHANDAS K. GANDHI

Connections

Connections are essential for a happy life. Connect to yourself, to nature, to God, and to others. Strive to form close, strong relationships with family members, friends, and colleagues. Fuel your passions, and find your soulmate.

Give love, create love, and receive love. Embrace commitment—feelings of permanence, longevity, and stability are important ingredients in a successful relationship. And remember that healthy, close, and supportive relationships will only serve to enrich your life, bring you joy, and make you feel happy!

An honest assessment of your innermost feelings and beliefs will help you live an authentic life. When you know yourself, you're more able to connect with others. Engage in physical activities, look after your health, and nurture your friendships. Discover your passions and hidden talents, and share them with others. Count your blessings and develop an appreciation of the special beauty that is present in even the most mundane and everyday things.

Turn wishful thinking into positive action. Those who take a proactive stance in their lives, who practice mindfulness, and pay attention to present-moment experiences, tend to have an ample supply of joy and pleasure.

Twenty years from now you will be more disappointed by the things that you didn't do than by the ones you did do. So throw off the bowlines. Sail away from the safe harbor. Catch the trade winds in your sails. Explore. Dream. Discover.

MARK TWAIN

"Kindness brings happiness. Kindness to oneself, kindness to others, kindness to other creatures. When someone is behaving kindly, I consider them my teacher, no matter their age." *Susan*

Let us be grateful to people who make us happy; they are the charming gardeners who make our souls blossom.

MARCEL PROUST

There is only one happiness in life, to love and be loved.

GEORGE SAND

"Connections are everything. My happy life is all about the closeness I have with my partner, family, and friends. It's taken me a lifetime to learn to tell the truth to myself and those I love about what I want and need, as I was conditioned to feel that was selfish. Happiness is about taking things off my plate, rather than adding them. It's having time and space to dream and breathe; being close rather than being right. Savoring sweet moments, trusting the tough times will pass." *Debbie*

Seek positive role models and learn
life-enhancing, esteem-building
behaviors from them.

*A friend is a gift
you give yourself.*

ROBERT LOUIS STEVENSON

Remember the Law of Attraction, and make an effort to attract positive, happy experiences into your life.

*The happiness of your life depends
upon the quality of your thoughts.*

MARCUS AURELIUS ANTONINUS

21

It is neither wealth nor splendor; but tranquility and occupation which give you happiness.

THOMAS JEFFERSON

Be true to yourself—be authentic.
Living mindfully simply means that you recognize
your present emotions without judging them.

Engage in a positive internal conversation.
Write in a journal, and tell yourself encouraging
and supportive stories about being you.

Independence is happiness.

SUSAN B. ANTHONY

The richness I achieve comes from Nature,
the source of my inspiration.

CLAUDE MONET

Wellbeing

MEDITATE ❁ DE-STRESS ❁ REJUVENATE

Take good care of yourself, mind and body. Take exercise—just thirty minutes a day will sharpen your problem-solving skills, and help to keep your body functioning to the best of its ability.

You can exercise your mind, too, by continuing to learn. Have faith in your ability to develop new skills, and learn from every experience, especially the challenging ones. Resist helplessness or blind acceptance of unpleasant circumstances. Although you can't change the facts of your life, you can change your perspective on those facts! A relaxed mental state will allow you to have an awareness of the present moment. And that, after all, is all we have.

Take responsibility for the quality of your life, and find a reason to enjoy every day. Be creative, and look for ways to be inspired.

Master a new skill. When you take the time to engage in activities that absorb your full attention, you'll experience a sense of wellbeing and contentment. These "flow" activities keep you in the present moment, and that's the place you want to be!

Live as if you were to die tomorrow.
Learn as if you were to live forever.

MAHATMA GANDHI

Live your life fully now. Seek out new experiences and bring mindful attention to daily tasks. Life is not a dress rehearsal. Use it before you lose it!

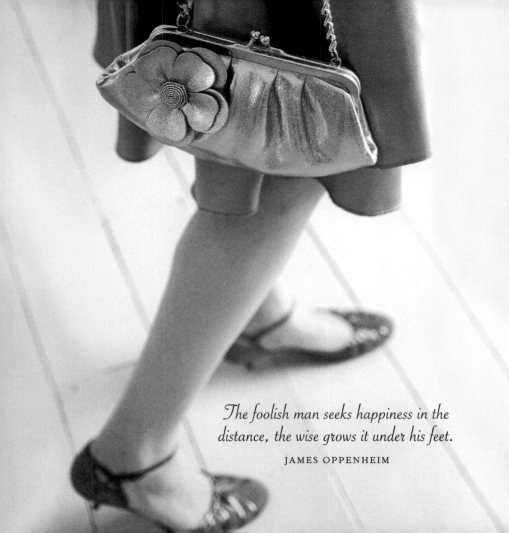

The foolish man seeks happiness in the distance, the wise grows it under his feet.

JAMES OPPENHEIM

The greatest part of our happiness depends
on our dispositions, not our circumstances.

MARTHA WASHINGTON

Use your natural gifts and talents.
Find ways to enhance your quality
of life with them.

Find your center—
a calm and content place
deep inside yourself—
and spend some time
there each day. If you
find this difficult, take a
course in mindfulness
meditation—you
won't regret it.

Hope is the thing with feathers—
That perches in the soul—
And sings the tune without the words—
And never stops—at all.

EMILY DICKINSON

Avoid false fixes.
Over-indulging in shopping, food, alcohol, or
drugs won't bring you happiness. Ask for help—
and seek positive coping skills instead.

Wisdom is the supreme part of happiness.

SOPHOCLES

Happiness comes when your work and words are of benefit to yourself and others.

BUDDHA

"The key to happiness for me is when those most important to me are happy. When I get to surprise my husband with his favorite ice cream from the store when he wasn't expecting it, when I take my daughter to the petting zoo when she wasn't expecting it, when I have a few minutes to sit on the couch and lounge with my pups and rub their bellies, when I tell my mom how my daughter has been asking to go visit her. Seeing the smiles, hearing the joy, seeing the tails wag... it's all pretty simple, but really is what makes my world go round." *Stacy*

Laugh out loud, robustly and often.
No one is in charge of your happiness but you!

*If only we'd stop trying to be happy,
we could have a pretty good time.*

EDITH WHARTON

Our greatest happiness does not depend on the condition of life in which chance has placed us, but is always the result of a good conscience, good health, occupation, and freedom in all just pursuits.

THOMAS JEFFERSON

Fill the cup of happiness for others, and there will be enough overflowing to fill yours to the brim.

ROSE PASTOR STOKES

Gratitude

Be grateful for the blessings you have, and at the same time be happy for others. This is not a competition—there is more than enough happiness to go around, once you know where to look. And besides, happiness is contagious, so make an effort to infect everyone around you.

Focus on the quality of your life, rather than the quantity—there are no guarantees. Look around you. Enjoy the simple yet miraculous things life has to offer. Find pleasure in the sunrise, and amazement in the moonlight. Be thrilled by the miracle of birth, and respectful of the power of nature. Be cognizant of the flora and fauna that exist on this earth, and appreciate the very air you breathe. Inhale the fragrance of flowers, and delight in the shade thrown by a tree. Perform random acts of kindness. You'll discover that gratitude and forgiveness are essential ingredients of a happy and fulfilled life.

"I was blessed to have my parents live with us for the past twenty years—a gift that enriched the lives of our entire family. We were able to be with them through the end of their lives—supporting them every step, to the very last breath. Celebrating life with them taught us all what it means to live a happy, mindful life. I wish the same for all of us." *Cheryl*

We don't receive wisdom; we must discover it for ourselves after a journey that no one can take for us or spare us.

MARCEL PROUST

Pay it forward. Give of your time, talent, and treasure to others in need, and practice random acts of kindness. These rewarding activities will start a cycle of generosity and make you feel really good!

The happiest people I have known have been those who gave themselves no concern about their own souls, but did their uttermost to mitigate the miseries of others.

ELIZABETH CADY STANTON

Holding a grudge is a waste of precious time. Everyone makes mistakes. If you hold on to a grudge, you're the one that suffers from anger and resentment. Forgive, forget it, and move on.

Forget the past and live the present hour.

SARAH KNOWLES BOLTON

Sing and hum. Read stories
about triumph over catastrophe,
of growth, progress, and
change for the better.

Always be a little kinder than necessary.

JAMES M. BARRIE

Practicing self-care is not selfish. Look after yourself, and you will have the energy to look after others. Try to eat reasonably well, get enough sleep, and walk! These may be simple instructions, but they are amazingly effective.

To be what we are, and to become what we are capable of becoming, is the only end of life.

ROBERT LOUIS STEVENSON

"Happiness is simply a choice in life. In each and every moment we experience, we can either make the best of it or the worst of it. The only moment we experience in reality is the present, and knowing that, we must always be fully focused on the present, as opposed to the past or future. Each person creates their own reality without thoughts and energy, so we must always focus on positivity and growing as a human." *Wesley*

The only truly happy man is always a fighting optimist.
Optimism includes not only altruism but also social responsibility,
social courage, and objectivity.

W. BERAN WOLFE

Thank God for your blessings,
tell the truth, and be proactive.

Happiness belongs to the self-sufficient.

ARISTOTLE

Do the tough stuff. Living an authentic life sometimes requires you to make hard choices. Find the courage to be the best you can be.

Whatever is—is best.

ELLA WHEELER WILCOX

A Recipe for
a Loving
Relationship

be patient ❀ RESPECT ONE ANOTHER

support your partner's passions

STAY CONNECTED ❀ find time to be sexy

be playful ❀ OPEN YOUR HEART

words can hurt—use them wisely

FORGIVE AND FORGET ❀ be generous with praise

remember patience is a virtue ❀ BE KIND

make time for quality time

SAY "I LOVE YOU" EVERY DAY

be compassionate as well as passionate

CULTIVATE PASTIMES YOU CAN ENJOY TOGETHER

take responsibility for your actions

KISS, HUG, AND TOUCH EACH OTHER OFTEN

protect your love with every beat of your heart

EXPRESS GOOD INTENTIONS ❀ be your best self

Marriage isn't ownership.
It's a partnership.

UNKNOWN

Partners

When two people make the decision to formalize their relationship, either by marriage, or by telling friends and family that this is the person they want to share their life with, it's a big deal. Even if you've been in a relationship for some time, the decision to make a formal commitment changes things up a bit. Just know that when you find yourself in this happy place, be grateful. You'll be sharing life with someone you deeply care for—someone who feels that way about you, too. A loving, strong relationship is a beautiful thing. You can tell when a couple has a strong connection. You can see it in their body language—the way they look at each other and the way they touch; the respect they have for each other and the affection they easily display.

When you can share your life with someone who enjoys the things you enjoy —someone who can laugh with you, be mindful of your feelings, and yes, stay sexy with you—and who also knows how important it is to maintain his or her individuality while at the same time cultivate a strong union as a couple, you have accomplished what most people on earth are striving for: a loving partnership. Protect it and nurture it with all your heart.

Love me when I least deserve it,
because that is when I really need it.

SWEDISH PROVERB

Love each other unconditionally. Having unrealistic expectations of your partner, trying to change them, or expecting perfection won't lead to happiness for either of you. Open your heart and your mind, without conditions or demands.

A good husband makes a good wife.

JOHN FLORIO

Opposites might attract,
but it's our similarities
that keep us together.

Let the husband render unto the wife due benevolence: and likewise also the wife unto the husband.

THE BIBLE, I CORINTHIANS 7:3

Practice acceptance. Sometimes it's wisest to simply agree to disagree. You're individuals after all, not clones.

"In his forties, my husband had a major mid-life crisis. He was distant, irritable, resentful. He felt the years had flown past and while he was being a good son, student, husband, and father there had been no space for him to find out who he was or what he wanted from life. He didn't want to be with me or spend time as a family and that hurt terribly. We stuck at it, tried to be kind, talked, listened, went to counseling, and gave each other space. It was tough, but very, very slowly things got better and we emerged from the storm with a new appreciation and understanding of each other. Relationships can be hard, but it's always worth fighting to save a good partnership." *Stephanie*

There is no more lovely,
friendly, and charming
relationship, communion,
or company than a
good marriage.

MARTIN LUTHER

Let go of judgment.
Learn to be tolerant
of your differences,
and respect them.

*You were born together, and together you
shall be forevermore... But let there be spaces in your togetherness,
And let the winds of the heavens dance between you.*

KAHLIL GIBRAN

Take care of each other. Share secrets. Create a private club with just the two of you in it.

A good marriage… is a sweet association in life:
Full of constancy, trust, and an infinite number of useful
and solid services and mutual obligations.

MICHEL DE MONTAIGNE

The supreme happiness in life is the assurance of
being loved for oneself, even in spite of oneself.

VICTOR HUGO

Don't lose yourself.
Remember why you
got together in the
first place.

Pause during conflict and think twice before you say something critical. If you can't find words that are compassionate and respectful, then silence is golden. Hurt feelings can take a long time to heal.

Kindness in women, not their beauteous looks,
Shall win my love.

WILLIAM SHAKESPEARE

A good marriage is that in which each appoints the other guardian of his solitude.

RAINER MARIA RILKE

Keep a place both physically and spiritually for yourself. Private time is important for everyone. In this busy world, give yourself the luxury of quiet time, to reflect, to meditate, to breathe, to think—to be calm. When you can rest, and feel mindfully in the moment—even briefly—you'll feel renewed, refreshed, and happier.

*Touch me, touch the palm of your
hand to my body as I pass.
Be not afraid of my body.*

WALT WHITMAN

Lovers

PLEASURE ❀ DESIRE ❀ TRUST

The feelings one experiences when in love can be overwhelming. Desire, physical attraction, trust, compatibility, the need for companionship—even unwanted feelings like jealousy can all come into play. What is it about this emotion that can thrill us one minute, and make us cry the next?

When you love someone, you want that person to be happy—and that means loving unconditionally. You don't want to hurt the other by abusing power, or by needing to always be "right." When in love, you become sensitive to the feelings of your loved one, and she or he becomes sensitive to yours. There is mutual trust. Your whole being is finely attuned and attached to your loved one, and your heart beats faster at the very thought of his or her touch.

There is equality in true love. Two hearts beating in a symbiotic rhythm —two lives meshed together in a virtual dance of cooperation, sensuality, passion, and the business of overcoming the everyday stuff of life. Long-term lovers find the time to look at each other with desire every day. It's up to you to cherish and sustain your love. Make the effort. You won't regret it.

"I feel blessed to be in a long-term, loving marriage. Something I discovered early on was that my husband and I were polar opposites in how we handled emotions. I wear my heart on my sleeve, while he compartmentalizes his feelings to the point where it could seem as though he doesn't care. It didn't take long for us to recognize that we needed to communicate our differences, and this honest communication is one of the things that has helped us remain madly in love all these years. I'm still the emotional one, and he's still the stoic, but he's incredibly understanding of me, and I know he's having the same feelings as I am, but is processing them differently, and that is OK." *Cheryl*

Develop and practice caring behaviors. Hold hands, give back rubs, and bring flowers to each other... just because.

As man and wife, being
two, are one in love.

WILLIAM SHAKESPEARE

Have fun
Thrill each other
Naked dancing
Masks
Feathers
Dress up
Be silly
Make love!

Set aside time to nurture your relationship. Life has become so busy—
everyone runs a mile a minute. With work, and kids, if you have them, and
exercise, taking care of your home, and family, and hobbies—soon you feel as
if there is no time left for you as a couple. And you need that time. Make the
effort to schedule a few focused hours for each other daily and weekly. Play
tennis, take a class together, have breakfast in bed on lazy Sundays, take
a walk around the neighborhood and hold hands. Reconnect, and give
each other a hug and a seriously good kiss.

Licence my roving hands, and let them go,
Before, behind, between, above, below.

JOHN DONNE

Come live with me, and be my love,
And we will some new pleasures prove
Of golden sands, and crystal brooks,
With silken lines, and silver hooks.

JOHN DONNE

Find time for an occasional weekend away. Stepping outside
your everyday routine can add spice to your life and give
you time to rediscover each other. If it's hard to plan a full
weekend, try a "staycation" where you take each other to
a local hotel for the night. Sometimes a little change like
a candlelit dinner out, a toss in a different bed, and a stroll
around a different block can reignite your spark.

Care for your love tenderly.
Love that is nurtured can last for ever…
and that's a long, long time.

94

I married my husband for life, not for lunch.

UNKNOWN

Remember to have date nights. Though we all have many obligations in life, take time regularly to be ALONE with each other.

How do I love thee? Let me count the ways.
I love thee to the depth and breadth and height
My soul can reach.

ELIZABETH BARRETT BROWNING

Candlelight… champagne… sex, sex, sex!
OK, we all know that sex isn't the only driver
of a loving relationship. But it is important. Why not
ignite that light and bring back the shivers and long love sessions?
Loving couples keep passion alive. So whether it takes a sensual
massage, champagne and beautiful sheets, or tossing
that cellphone out of the room and really
being present—get your sexy on!

Marriage has many pains, but celibacy has no pleasures.

SAMUEL JOHNSON

When love has melted and mingled two beings into an angelic and sacred unity, the secret of life is found for them... they are then but the two wings of a single spirit. Love, soar!

VICTOR HUGO

Keeping a romance alive can be difficult if you find yourself competing with technical gadgets all the time. Phones, tablets, and other devices are no substitute for human, physical contact. Take time to look into each other's eyes, listen attentively to each other, be present in the moment without distractions. It feels really good.

Communicate!
Communicate!
Communicate!

Friends

Some of us would claim that friends are among life's greatest gifts. I believe we would be lost without them. When you are in a long-term relationship that is not only romantic and passionate, but also a friendship, you've accomplished a mighty feat. Friends listen—they let you vent, and explain, and complain without judging you. They give you an opportunity to be you. They're your biggest fan, your strongest supporter, your life raft, oxygen mask, and safe harbor in a storm.

Being in a relationship that works requires playtime. Everyone needs to relax, chill out, laugh, and have fun. During these trying times—and trust me, these are trying times—be mindful of the fact that we need to have laughter in our lives. The ability to be playful—to relax, to giggle, tease, and have fun—affects the quality of our relationships, and the quality of our lives, too. Find time to be a playmate in your relationship. Not only will you feel younger and more alive, you'll be living mindfully, happily, joyfully in the moment. And that's what friends are for!

Matrimony; the high sea for which no compass has yet been invented.

HEINRICH HEINE

Pick fights carefully.
Unless it's worth a divorce,
GIVE IT UP.
Life is too short!

Be to their virtue very kind;
be to their faults a little blind.

MATTHEW PRIOR

Don't take anything
too seriously, and
keep talking! The
"silent treatment"
doesn't work.

Never go to bed angry… stay up all night and
fight! Just kidding. Fighting isn't the answer. If you
can stay in the moment, recognize that you both have
your own point of view, and deal with the current issue with an
open mind and heart, instead of bringing up past hurts, you'll
be communicating like two adults who love each other.
Take a breath, count to ten, and shift your
attitude back to one of kindness.

The quality of a marriage is proven by its ability to tolerate an occasional "exception".

FRIEDRICH NIETZSCHE

Of all serious things, marriage is the funniest.

PIERRE DE BEAUMARCHAIS

Be present for what your partner is saying without the need
to solve his or her problems. Sit still, relax, focus, and listen.
Oftentimes we just need an empathetic listening ear rather
than advice or practical solutions.

Be willing to communicate, and then negotiate. Loving partners
will occasionally have differences—that's life. But if you want a
relationship to last, you'll recognize that the end goal is for both
parties to be happy. Forcing your partner to do something, or insisting
that your way is best, will only cause resentment. Be considerate.
Tell your truth honestly and calmly and then negotiate a compromise
fairly, so that you both feel good about it in the end.

The best friend will probably get the best spouse, because a good marriage is based on the talent for friendship.

FRIEDRICH NIETZSCHE

Marriage is the highest state of friendship:
If happy, it lessens our cares by dividing
them, at the same time that it doubles our
pleasures by mutual participation.

SAMUEL RICHARDSON

Make love, connect, talk, respect, and stand by your
man and/or woman… and expect him or her to
stand by you. A long-lasting, loving relationship is
like a garden that needs constant tending to grow. It
isn't hard work; it is satisfying, heartfelt work that
feels good, and fills you with a kind of
joy that is connected to the divine.

Cultivate love. Many of us yearn to be swept away on a wave of romance, but don't devote any time to nurturing our feelings for our partner. Gaze into his or her eyes. Appreciate their good qualities. Practice loving thoughts, patience, and compassion.

Keep your eyes wide open before marriage, half shut afterwards.

BENJAMIN FRANKLIN

In marriage do thou be wise;
prefer the person before money;
virtue before beauty;
the mind before the body.

WILLIAM PENN

"When my first marriage failed, I was crushed. I was surrounded by happily married friends with small kids living in nuclear family units and I felt like the odd one out, the failure. I was terribly wounded and it took five years before I could even entertain the thought of going on a date. Well, it turns out that good things do come to those who wait. My second husband is the kindest, most generous man I have ever met. We love reading and traveling and chatting and movies, and he makes me laugh so much. Every single day, I am thankful for my great good fortune in finding him." *Christa*

A Recipe for a
Strong Sisterhood

stay in touch ❀ NOURISH CLOSE RELATIONSHIPS

share your deepest desires

TAKE A CREATIVE ADVENTURE TOGETHER

howl at the moon ❀ SUPPORT EACH OTHER

leave judgment at the door

BE A GOOD LISTENER ❀ *make time for friends*

go camping together ❀ EMBRACE YOUR DIFFERENCES

celebrate motherhood, sisterhood, womanhood

RECOGNIZE YOUR INNER BEAUTY

cherish your girlfriends ❀ *be proud of your strength*

UNDERSTAND THE HARD TIMES

pray and dance ❀ HUG EACH OTHER

ADMIT YOUR VULNERABILITY ❀ *be loyal*

tell your story ❀ ACKNOWLEDGE YOUR COURAGE

be kind ❀ LOVE EACH OTHER ❀ *choose happiness*

Truly great friends are hard to find,
difficult to leave, and impossible to forget.

UNKNOWN

Socializing and Connecting

SHARE ❋ LAUGH ❋ CRY

We share secrets with our girlfriends, we laugh with our girlfriends, and we cry with our girlfriends. We might even have the occasional argument with our girlfriends—hey, we're only human! But when we calm down and make up, we often become even closer afterwards.

We women bare our souls, share our emotions, and talk about the intimate details of our lives with our girlfriends. They are the ones we turn to when we need to vent about our relationships, complain about our kids, and cry about our disappointments, because we know they'll understand. Girlfriends are our cohorts, confidantes, role models, and support system. They understand our mood swings, and let us yammer on about the same gnarly subject that has us troubled until we get it out of our system... something the men in our lives may not be capable of doing.

Girl buddies help us moderate stress and lessen the sorrows that inevitably occur during our life journeys. A group of girlfriends is a commune we build among ourselves. We need it—our own special place and time.

"Girlfriends are my family... the family I have chosen! They are reliable, caring, fun, consistently there for me, and for their other friends, too. I could not live without them." *Martha*

Girlfriend time is therapeutic.
It can actually improve your health,
and help you live better.

Wishing to be friends is quick work,
but friendship is a slow-ripening fruit.

ARISTOTLE

"I met my girlfriends after I got married. We started a canasta group, and there were eight of us, all good friends. We were always there for each other. We had pot-luck dinners at each other's houses, and we babysat each other's kids so we'd get a chance to go out once in a while. The older you get, the more you appreciate your friends, because now some of them are gone. I still remember those that are gone, and all the good times we had together." *Betty*

"There doesn't seem to be an age limit on having fun with girlfriends. When we get a chance to be together for a ski or yoga trip—which is rare, because of kids and careers and husbands and homes and all the other responsibilities of our busy lives—we laugh like schoolgirls. Our hearts are light, and we let ourselves go. Love bounces around like light, and there is a special kind of warmth and glow around us that lightens us. This light and warmth lasts a long time. We all draw from the fountain of youth on a trip like that. Girlfriend-bonding time is like breathing giggle gas. It makes you smile." *Lynn*

Go on an adventure together.
Take a vacation, a dance class, pottery lessons,
or learn to play poker. Let your little girl out to play,
and have fun. It's never too late to be young at
heart with your girlfriends.

"I was once invited to a rather unique 'girls' dinner party. My friend, the hostess, was a little secretive about the reason for the party, but she did mention that it was going to be a bit naughty. Little did I know! We had margaritas first, then gathered around a table with an expert who brought in a display of sex toys and showed us how to use them! We all got a chance to show off our various skills, and we laughed until we cried. We had the best time together and, of course, we vowed to keep the details confidential. Oh, how we laughed. We could only imagine what our men would have given to be a fly on the wall that night! It was a memorable evening—one that this group of girlfriends will long remember!" *Anonymous*

Giggle like schoolgirls, share secrets,
laugh and be silly. The pure enjoyment
of being with a friend will brighten
and lighten your day.

Be a good listener. Pay attention,
and actually focus on what your girlfriend
is saying. It's not your job to fix your girlfriend's
problems, but try to listen attentively, respectfully,
and without judgment so that she can feel
heard, supported, and validated.

"My godmother, my second mother, has been a blessing in my life and
the key to mindfulness for me. Her positive attitude, her willingness
and ability to put her wants and needs second is what makes her special.
I see how much she cares for people when she speaks with them; she
makes each one feel like they are the most important person in the
world. And, whatever she does, she does fully and with immense
passion. She is my inspiration." *Ari*

*It's not so much our
friends' help that helps
us, as the confidence
of their help.*

EPICURUS

"My heart races when I think about my girlfriends. I can't wait to see them, and I feel that we are invincible when we're together. I couldn't live my life without mine. That's what soul sisters are all about." *Irena*

"We are a group of five sisters-in-law and friends that are very close. We laugh, we cry, and we take vacations together. The most important memory for me was how my friends rallied around me when I went through my mother's illness and passing. They took care of my kids and my house. They brought food to the hospital, they prayed and cried with me, and helped me to accept and make the hardest decision of my life. Afterwards, they helped me remember my mother in a positive way. Our group enjoys getting together, so we have what we call 'stress-reliever Fridays.' We talk about our kids and the men in our lives, we drink wine, we might even sing karaoke! We are there for each other. We call ourselves *"Las Comadres."* This is the name in Spanish for someone who is the godparent of your child. We have all become godmothers of each other's kids. And, after all this time, we still have too much fun!" *Isabel*

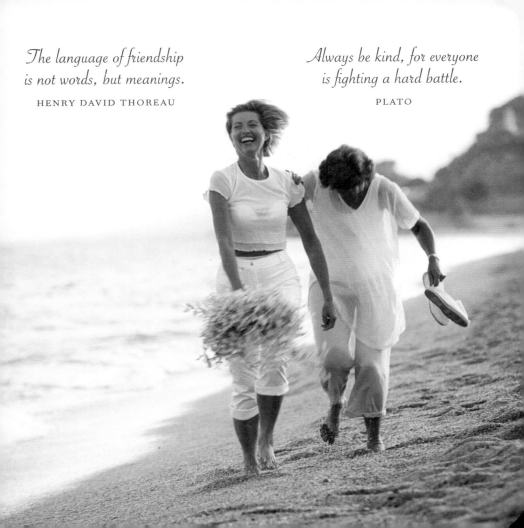

*The language of friendship
is not words, but meanings.*

HENRY DAVID THOREAU

*Always be kind, for everyone
is fighting a hard battle.*

PLATO

Friends show their love in times of trouble.

EURIPEDES

Nuturing and Celebrating

GET TOGETHER ❦ ENGAGE ❦ CONNECT

The importance of nurturing female friendships cannot be taken lightly. Long-lasting ties with girlfriends can make and keep us healthier. This is not wishful thinking—it's backed up by research and study. Those sweet moments spent chatting over tea and cake are actually good for our health and wellbeing—perhaps as good as spending time in the gym.

While we all benefit from technology and the ability to stay connected 24/7, make an effort to meet face-to-face. Yes, texting is great, and email, and other social networking options—they've opened up a whole world of ways for us to stay in touch. However, try to get upfront and personal whenever possible. There's nothing like physical contact to reinforce the closeness we crave.

Girlfriend get-togethers allow us to share deeper parts of ourselves. The smiles, laughter, and the actual warmth of the hugs you'll receive make it well worth the effort of carving out some precious girlfriend time. But if you can only manage phone calls and emails, then do that. Just stay connected.

Nurture and celebrate one another, because it's all good.

Friendships, like gardens, need some tender loving
care and attention in order to grow. With girlfriends, as with
all relationships, this requires a subtle dance of give and take,
but not one of keeping score or tit for tat. Enjoy what you
receive, and then enjoy giving back as well. Nurture and
cultivate your friendships.

"I had one of my greatest challenges in my life over fifteen years ago—a time when I really needed my friends' support, and this is what I discovered: True girlfriends are the ones who stand by you in your darkest hour. While others walk away, a select few march toward you and become even closer friends. They are there through the good, the bad, and the ugly. They nurture you and love you, asking for nothing in return." *Barbara*

"My soul-sister girlfriends mean the world to me. They listen to your every word and care about what you are saying. They never judge you and they are always there for you, especially when you need them the most." *Vanna*

"I never realized how special a soul sister could be until I met my soon-to-be husband. He has a sister-in-law that I will be inheriting along with the rest of his wonderful family. She and I have a very special connection. We both grew up with brothers and married into a family of all boys. I like to think that we each fill a sisterly void that we never knew we had. We laugh for hours, go on adventures, and truly care about each other. We now share the bond of family and, even though it's not blood, I love her as if it were. There is something extraordinary in realizing that even if you weren't born with a sister you will find her, one way or another, along the way." *Jordyn*

Offer advice with compassion; accept advice with grace. We only truly know what we know about ourselves. Our opinions and recommendations are one perspective: Our own. It's not up to us to be judge and jury—we're there to be honest, openhearted, and kind.

Hold a true friend
with both hands.

NIGERIAN PROVERB

"My girlfriends are like the perfect diamond—
multifaceted, hard to find, difficult to give up,
impossible to forget, and absolutely priceless.
Couldn't live without them." *Lovey*

"When I was a kid, my mom's favorite quote was 'The art of living is more like wrestling than dancing,' from the Greek emperor Marcus Aurelius. Girlfriends help your heart and soul sing, whether it's your time to wrestle or dance. They are there whether you need them or not. Girlfriends are like sisters without all the baggage." *Jeanne*

Friends are an important part of our lives—they bring us joy and a sense of community. They lift us up when we're down, they give us hugs when we're sad, and they're our cheerleaders for the good times in our lives. Though it may not be possible to maintain a close relationship with all the women you meet, if you really cannot get along with someone, then at least withdraw your "cat claws" and be mature about it. Life is too short to hold on to anger. Nurture the friends you enjoy, and try to learn lessons from everyone who steps into your path.

*Blessed is the influence of one true,
loving human soul on another.*

GEORGE ELIOT

"Girlfriends best be chosen wisely. Girlfriends need to be bountiful, not plentiful; protective secret-keepers who pull you up and sometimes back. They tell you the truth. They tether you when your moorings are loose, and happily celebrate your flying. They love you. And you need to be a girlfriend back—it's a reciprocal relationship." *Gail*

It is one of the blessings of old friends that you can afford to be stupid with them.

RALPH WALDO EMERSON

"Emotional bonds with a girlfriend can navigate both time and space. You may live in different cities, even on different continents, but your friendship won't be shaken. I have a friendship like that. We've both found that a phone call, an email, or a hand-written letter can reach across the expanse and bring warmth and a deep, abiding sentiment that resonates with pleasure for us both. Such a friendship is a treasure indeed." *Cheryl*

*A true friend is one who knows
when there's something wrong,
even if you have the biggest
smile on your face.*

UNKNOWN

*Nothing but heaven itself is better than
a friend who is really a friend.*

PLAUTUS

Comforting and Tending

LISTEN ❀ UNDERSTAND ❀ SUPPORT

The special relationship of girlfriends is a phenomenon that we as women have long understood and relished, but that scientists have only recently begun to analyze in earnest. The reason being a simple, yet critical one— girlfriends are good for our health! And there is another, perhaps even more intriguing fact—maintaining and nurturing friendships may actually protect us against life-threatening illness. That's something worth clucking about.

Whatever the specialists say, women the world over certainly know that having close girlfriends brings joy into our lives. Make time for them. Resist the urge to put them on the back-burner when life gets overwhelming because that is precisely when you need your girlfriends the most.

Put on the kettle or chill a bottle of wine, or grab your yoga mat, your surfboard, your jogging shoes, your knitting, your cookie dough, or whatever catnip you need to inspire you to rally round your girlfriends and just let girlfriend-comfort time begin. And then repeat. Again and Again. See? Even the thought of your gal pals can make you smile.

One good heart attracts another.
Each true friend deserves the other.

SHAKER SAYING

*Friends are angels who lift us to our feet when our
wings have trouble remembering how to fly.*

UNKNOWN

"Spiritual connections are conditional on our openness and readiness to accept them. I bonded with like-minded girls as a teenager when we joined a group called *Habonim* (The Builders), to collect money for UNICEF. We found such joy in each other, no matter what our economic status or physical appearances. My own sister, six years older than me, was always in a different place, and it took many years before we connected. We are now so close, and laugh, share, and cry together. I feel so lucky. I am still close to those girls from my teenage years. They are my lifelong soul sisters. Plus, I have my 'blood' sister, who, to my great surprise, has become a soul sister, too!" *Sue*

"Years ago, I had a serious cancer scare. The morning I was scheduled for surgery, one of my dearest girlfriends took me to the hospital to check me into the cancer center. My husband, who was usually so strong, had gotten freaked out about the whole thing and decided to skip the preliminaries and come to the hospital just before I went into the operating room. I understood. My girlfriend and I would handle the fear and emotion of it all in a different way, as women do. I was scared but trying to be brave. While I got prepped for surgery, my girlfriend was by my side. She was a steady, loving force, holding my hand, calming me, helping me find my inner courage. She kept me breathing in a regular pattern, and reminded me to focus on the positive outcome I was praying for. In the end, I was one of the lucky ones, and I am fine… cancer free. This girlfriend is still one of my dearest, most steadfast friends, and I will always be grateful for her strength and love during some of my darkest hours." *Charlyn*

Girlfriend time is good for your
health, mentally and physically.
Do your best to make time for it.

Everywhere, we learn only from those whom we love.

JOHANN WOLFGANG
VON GOETHE

"Soon after I moved to the West Coast, I met a group of women who all became fast friends. One friend in particular has become one of my closest girlfriends. We had our weddings within months of each other. We had our children in the same years. Unfortunately, she relocated back to the Midwest. But this hasn't put a dent in our relationship. If anything, it has grown stronger. No distance will get in the way of our friendship. I wish we were able to do weekly dinners, but we are certainly not going to let a little bit of a location issue interfere with our sisterhood. It is the presence of friends like this that makes me a better person. Her words and counsel help put the little hiccups in life in perspective. We remind each other that our children are not out of the ordinary, that our relationships are not perfect but still worth working on, that our careers are on the right track. We support each other in the good times and the bad. We make each other laugh and cry. And we wish the best for one another—unconditional love that transcends time and space. I am very lucky." *Marni*

"Years ago, I was going through a particularly difficult period, but was reluctant to share anything about it. I thought it was too personal—it concerned someone in my family, a child, who was dealing with a terrible illness—and though I trusted my girlfriends, I didn't have the energy to reach out to them. I was consumed by sadness, and I became a hermit. One day, I went to a hair salon, trying to keep up appearances by doing everyday things. Two of my best girlfriends showed up while I was sitting there, staring into space, numb and despondent. They wrapped their arms around me and I dissolved into tears—something I desperately needed to do. They sat with me, helping me cope, bringing me back to a place of strength and courage. My girlfriends are selfless, intuitive angels—they were my Rock of Gibraltar when I needed them to be." *Flora*

*The only way to have
a friend is to be one.*

RALPH WALDO EMERSON

Being deeply loved by someone gives you strength, while loving someone deeply gives you courage.

LAO TZU

"The truest friend holds a mirror to our soul and sees the spark that lives in our heart. I can trust her with all of me, knowing that the times I may not like what I see inside myself, she is always there to remind me that I am not alone. I will have her love to sustain me when I find it hard to nourish myself. She is my rock, my laughter, the beauty in all things, hope, and a safe haven that, in the changing reality of time, always remains constant and true. She is love." *Lili*

Girlfriends are intuitive They pick up on each other's emotional needs. Sometimes, just being present is enough.

"I had a dear girlfriend who stayed close despite weeks, or even months, without us seeing each other. Once, we even endured a year of separation and only communicated sporadically. Yet the special link between us remained sacrosanct. We 'got' each other, like no one else could. When we did have the chance to get together in person, we would pick up where we left off, as though we had never been apart. We gave each other advice, talked about our kids, the men in our lives, our careers—everything and anything. She's gone now, but I have memories that I will always cherish. The unique friendship we shared touched me deeply, and her essence will be wrapped around my heart for as long as I live." *Taylor*

When you're with your girlfriend, you know
you're in a safe harbor, and you can be yourself.

Picture Credits

1 www.davidaustinroses.com. ph Debi Treloar 2 www.yeabridgehouse.com. ph Debi Treloar 3 ph Polly Wreford 4 ph Rachel Whiting 5 www.vintagebynina.com. ph Lisa Cohen 6 Hôtel Le Sénéchal, Ars en Ré. ph Paul Massey 8 ph Polly Wreford 10 www.beachstudios.co.uk. ph Polly Wreford 12 ph Paul Massey 13 ph Paul Ryan 14 ph Claire Richardson 15 ph Debi Treloar 16 www.tse-tse.com. ph Debi Treloar 17 ph Claire Richardson 18 ph William Lingwood 19 ph Claire Richardson 20 ph Tom Leighton 21 Le Clos du Lethe. ph Claire Richardson 22 ph Debi Treloar 23–24 ph Polly Wreford 25–26 ph Claire Richardson 28 ph Polly Wreford 29 ph Paul Massey 30 ph Polly Wreford 31 ph Claire Richardson 32 ph Paul Massey 33 www.tresanton.com. ph Paul Massey 34 ph Chris Tubbs 35 ph Debi Treloar 36 ph Claire Richardson 37 ph Jonathan Gregson 38 kali9/Getty Images 39 ph Peter Cassidy 40 ph Claire Richardson 41 Mathilde Labrouche of Cote Pierre's home in Saintonge. From Recycled Home by Mark and Sally Bailey. ph Debi Trelaor 42 ph Chris Everard 43 ph Peter Cassidy 44 ph Claire Richardson 46–47 ph Polly Wreford 48–49 ph Lisa Cohen 50 ph James Merrell 51 ph Polly Wreford 52 www.olelynggaard.com. ph Paul Massey 53 ph Martin Brigdale 54 ph Emma Mitchell 55 ph Paul Massey 56–57 Mark and Sally Bailey's home in Herefordshire. From *Simple Home* by Mark & Sally Bailey. Ph Debi Treloar 58 ph Debi Treloar 59 ph Paul Massey 60 ph James Merrell 61 ph Paul Massey 62 ph Polly Wreford 64 ph Dan Duchars 66–67 ph Jo Henderson 68 ph Andrew Wood 69 ph James Merrell 70–71 Debi Treloar 72 ph Polly Wreford 73 ph Dan Duchars 74 www.botelet.com. ph Jan Baldwin 75 ph James Merrell 76 ph Caroline Arber 77 ph Jo

Henderson 78 ph Sandra Lane 79 ph Debi Treloar 80 ph Sandra Lane 81 ph Debi Treloar 82 ph Viv Yeo 83–84 ph Polly Wreford 86 ph Viv Yeo 87 ph Catherine Gratwicke 88 ph Polly Wreford 89 ph Caroline Arber 90 ph Peter Cassidy 91 Home of Tim Rundle and Glynn Jones. ph Debi Treloar 92 ph Chris Tubbs 93 ph Earl Carter 94 ph Gavin Kingcome and Claire Richardson 95 www.davidaustinroses.com. ph Debi Treloar 96 ph Debi Treloar 97 ph William Lingwood 98 ph Debi Treloar 99 ph Polly Wreford 100 ph Daniel Farmer 101 ph Polly Wreford 102–104 ph Caroline Arber 105 ph Debi Treloar 106 ph Polly Wreford 107 www.lillagrona.se. ph Rachel Whiting 108–109 ph Polly Wreford 110 ph Caroline Arber 111 ph Polly Wreford 112 ph Mark Scott 113 ph Dan Duchars 114–115 ph Polly Wreford 116 ph David Brittain 117 ph Daniel Farmer 118 www.sophieconran. com. ph Catherine Gratwicke 119 ph Polly Wreford 120 Peathegee Inc/Getty Images 122 ph Dan Duchars 124 bikeriderlondon/ Shutterstock.com 125 www.lavender-room. co.uk. ph Debi Treloar 126 ph Polly Wreford 127 ph Debi Treloar 129 Westend 61/Getty Images 130–133 ph Debi Treloar 134 monkeybusinessimages/Getty Images 135 ph Debi Treloar 137 ph www.arendal-ceramics.com. ph Debi Treloar 138 ph Christopher Drake 139 Benelux/Corbis/VCG/Getty Images 140 ph Sandra Lane 142-143 ph Claire Richardson 144 ph Debi Treloar 145 www.strommafarmlodge. com. ph Rachel Whiting 147 JGalione/Getty Images 148 ph Claire Richardson 149 ph Debi Treloar 150 ph Dan Duchars 151 ph Ian Wallace 152–153 ph Polly Wreford 154–155 www.lavender-room.co.uk. ph Debi Treloar 156 ph Catherine Gratwicke 158 ph Sandra Lane 159 Alys Tomlinson/Getty Images 160 ph Peter Cassidy 163 monkeybusinessimages/Getty Images 164 ph Debi Treloar 167 Blasius Erlinger/Getty Images 168 ph Polly Wreford 171 ph Debi Treloar 172 ph Polly Wreford 175 ph Debi Treloar

Acknowledgments

I am deeply grateful to my husband, children, and grandchildren
who surround me with love and contribute mightily to the delight,
joy, and contentment of my life. I am genuinely happy, and while
I know I am in great part responsible for my own happiness, they
are certainly one of the reasons I can wake up every day with a
smile on my face. I am also incredibly grateful that my parents
lived with us until the time of their passing. Their presence
in our lives was a blessing to us all.
I am so fortunate to have a large circle of friends, and am indebted
to those who generously shared life stories with me for this book.
And finally, a warm virtual hug to my editor, Annabel Morgan,
who is not only fun to work with, but has become
a delightfully caring, long-distance friend.